MW00895618

HERE I AM

Calvin Brown

Email: Sephrium @outlook.com

 FriesenPress

One Printers Way
Altona, MB R0G 0B0
Canada

www.friesenpress.com

ISBN
978-1-03-915873-3 (Hardcover)
978-1-03-915872-6 (Paperback)
978-1-03-915874-0 (eBook)

1. POETRY, CANADIAN

Distributed to the trade by The Ingram Book Company

Poems

Dearest reader,

Here I Am is a meant to rekindle the soul in all of us and awaken us from darkness.

This collection of poems and songs is to inspire and defeat many obstacles that have come my way in many forms.

Let these lessons and words help those who are suffering from many things, and say you are not alone.

Let them give you the ability to overcome and share with those who just need to hear and not fear the past or the future.

Strive for your dreams no matter what is holding you back.

Take courage and battle those who do not seem to care.

Many are waiting for your voice to be heard.

Calvin Brown

YOU SHY AWAY

Would you take?
A gentle Kiss.
Could I make?
A thoughtful Gift.
I need you!

Would you know me?
Would you come?
I found Love.
I know Prayers.

To my days,
I say…
We can be free
Like the Jewel.
I have no pearl to hide.

We can be free.
Hold on for me.

We are love
We are one.
I see our day.
You shy away.

WHO IS THIS MAN?

Who is this man?
Who stares without interest.
Back from the glass.
It seems hideous, grotesque.
At times monstrous.
Lingering between swollen eyes,
Rotting skin.
The soul's true character is naked.

I turned away from the formation.
Once so beautiful, strong, and new.
How a young man's youth is painfully quick.
If I had been given a little more insight
into tomorrow.
Just a fraction of King Solomon's soulful gold.

Perhaps I was so blind.
I walked along the church pathways.
It seems so far off now.

I would have been King of my own destiny.
I would be able to stand the thought.
Of the rising morning.
But alas!
I am a lost Tyrant.
Drunk and abused.

My soul has become the battleground,
For the Angelic and the lost.
Making me pay for every thought,
Action, and crime.
That I once believed to be glorious tales.
Told to barmaids and friends.

Where do the lonely-hearted seek peace?
How do the sinful find true redemption?
Would that God's redemption could find me soon.
For I am sensing my undoing.
I see my own date of death.
I feel my own tomb!

VII

Who broke my looking glass?
Time?
Lies?
Or dreams?

Resting on a sandy beach.
The gulls screech.
But not my name.

Drunk on emptiness.
Drudgery is hypnotic.
Adrift one goes.
Extravagant one stays.

VIRGIN

A mistress
Of
Devilish brood.
Walked the road she did.
Ran.
She did eventually.
Thinking of the aching mind.

Laughing!
At neglected existence.
Ransomed and battered.
Was the heart.

Democracy!
Was an unseen storm.
Married the soul!
Disarranged isolation,
Amused a citizen like a fool.

WHAT DO ANGELS DREAM?

What do Angels dream?
Love makes them swift.
A place of rapture.

I am told to look away.
Surrendered to sleep.
Please stay with me…

I see my fallen foes.
Tarnished away.
Are they truly happy or tied to lies?
The body dies.

What do Angels dream.
Grey leaves,
She loved harp-filled hymns.
We try to be.
I am a beautiful picture.
So, they tell me
You are lies.
Walking to the edge,
Suicide?
Trapped in revenge.
Lost in remorse
Would you like to play the game?
You will never know my name.

It hurts so bad!
Cuts and mutilates.
Transparent but rusty!
Sequestered.
Longing days.

What do Angels dream.
Mystic horn.
Skin soft.
If I could only be…
Adored and kissed
Our days are done.

Lovers sing.
We run…
The dead scream!
Look into the framework of the sun.
We are found
I am free.

RED WOLF

When the orgies are finally over.
The call of the Raven is finally understood.
Across the landscape of time.
Black cars.
Painted faces,
Are no more.
Will the son of man?
Take much needed rest.

A Break from creation.
With a realization.
How lost are we really?

Dancing in the fire.
To worship the Sun and Moon.
An eclipse of such grief.
Words of the past,
Are a defiled echo of tomorrow.

Lend me a moment.
Just listen to Adam's broken heart.
Eve's first scream of birth.
When at last all was naked.

These are the sounds.
Of missing children in the night.
A drunken shuffle at a lowly bar.

Lost warriors in a grave.
Herds of Buffalo.
Disappeared from a gifted plain.

How is the sound of the dawn?
Your New Age.
Red wolf shoots
His arrows into the future.
With fury!

A shower within the moon.
With my brothers
On guard to war.
Turned to open and closing of doors.

Keys to be found
I cannot escape this night.

Between the mockery.
I declare I have nothing.
But a worn-out hammer.
Laid to rest.
Beside a dull wooden arrow.

For Adam's sin is our game.

WATER WELL (SONG)

By Calvin & Jason Brown

A Chance to speak the truth.
In a world that wants nothing else.
So let me dig a water well,
To Hell.

VERSE 1

I'm looking through
The eyes of our children
What are we doing living
When there is no true giving.

Every book
I read in school,
Nothing but war,
The Middle East is in a constant uproar.
And the good US of A
Blacks and Whites
Still do not know what to say.
Throughout the UK
Old tribes so entwined
In a flamboyant Monarchy of design.

I am really trying to stand.
Searching for answers for Man.
Digging in so deep
That my mind won't let me sleep
What else can we do from here
In a world caught up in fear.

CHORUS

This is for the people now!
Do you hear me now?
Do you hear me know?

This is for the people now!
Do you hear me now?
Do you hear me know?

Let's kiss these tales goodbye
So no more children have to cry.
I would rather die!
Then continue to live your lies.

God can you hear the cries of your children?
God can you hear the cries of your children?

For only a fool says there is no God.
MY GOD

VERSE 2

Different feelings lead to peaceful talks
Different strokes for everybody
Means it's time to walk.
Anticipation leads to mistakes at haste.
So slow down and understand
There is no time to waste.

Flavor tastes good on the mouths of fools
So savor true knowledge
Study the rules.
The eyes hold the pain of mistakes
 from the past.
Eyes of the stranger means it's time to blast.

Orders and levels come to wishful thinking.
Then we all look to this sky
No time for sinking
Or blinking cause so much is to be seen
So I look on and feel the redeemed.

CHORUS

This is for the people now!
Do you hear me now?
Do you hear me know?

This is for the people now!
Do you hear me now?

Do you hear me know?

Let's kiss these tales goodbye
So no more children have to cry.
I would rather die!
Then continue to live your lies.

God can you hear the cries of your children?
God can you hear the cries of your children?

For only a fool says there is no God.
MY GOD

VERSE 3

This is for the people you know.
This is for the believers to show
(My God, My God, My God).
Can you not feel the pain of each other.
I throw a high five cause that's my brother.

We continue to cast out sinners without love
Why does the merciful one look down from above?

Messages wrapped up with hateful intent
Why street talkers and walkers can't pay the rent.

We need a place to come together.
Conjunctional efforts that make things better.

Please tell me when is enough enough.
Save some love before it gets too much.

CHORUS

This is for the people now!
Do you hear me now?
Do you hear me know?

This is for the people now!
Do you hear me now?
Do you hear me know?

Let's kiss these tales goodbye
So no more children have to cry.
I would rather die!
Then continue to live your lies.

God can you hear the cries of your children?
God can you hear the cries of your children?

For only a fool says there is no God.
MY GOD

TWO PLAYS

Lesser Evils,
I am fame!
The last of Pagan days.
A peaceful joy.

We are strong.
Grace unknown.
Give m a visitor.
Let me know your name!

See these…

GOD
ANGELS
ADAM

SATAN
FALLEN
MAN

Take me down,
To bury my only gift.
A free loving soul!

We are what is life!
For shame,
Tearful eyed shame…

WALL

The wall boldly stands.
In a servant's path.
Its bricks keep him at bay.

Eagles rest on its view.
Crows scream damnation.

To get through.
The servant can only dream.
What lies beyond the wall?

He climbs and strains.
Fingers buried.
In deep Stone.
So alone.
He cannot see
His abode.

THE UTOPIANS

The visionaries stood detached.
Staring over treetops.
Hearts dissatisfied.
Ideas of change.
Hath turned to rage

The Utopians.
Who dreamed of peace?
Love thy neighbor.
Fornicate oneself.

Soiling the church
Burning flags.
Rehabilitated
Left prisoners,
With no escape.

One parent family.
Left once joyfully
Children in agony
With a dismantled
Political hierarchy.
They left us with Anarchy.

THE SHOW

It is so profound.
This Shallow legend.
Turn it off.

Amusement is below par.
Broke off.
Dejected,
For the slightest
Characters laugh.
Apathetic for tears.

Just turn it off.
I cannot!
Addicted to this uproar,
Of alienated dialogue
A growing script of turmoil.
That holds me to weep.

As the final curtain
Folds along the bowing,
Crossed arms.
I have found sanctity and rewards.
For its honesty and plight.
It moves me to look.
Across the crowd.

Some of the faces knew,
The uplifting outcome
Others feared for the worse.
While a few just stared unconcerned.
As if it was just another show.

CAPTIVE

I foresaw,
A mountain of bones.
Marvel!
Would I ever touch the sea?

I walked along a path of glory
Unaltered
I was just a dream.

Rooms of others.
Duration!
For the likes of me.

The lethargic.
Whispered…
Amongst themselves.

The frames of deception.
Embrace!
An arm's length of love.

I awoke along a river's edge.
Peace!
Who took my dreams?

Surely
I am captive to her words.
I am alone.

LONGING

I know how Adam felt.
When he was first deceived.
How we both still grieve.
Lord
Harden this festering
Tenderness in my heart.

To my dear departed brother.
I must tell you I tried.
To plant your seed as mine.
Watch it grow in time.
Alas
Only God!
Must truly know of my trials.

To the heartless charlatans.
Of this decaying world.
Mere wealth is more than gold.
To be exposed.
We receive vinegar
Instead of aged wine.

Soon it will be our time.
Arise

THE ANIMAL ELITE

The Animal Elite.
Met at the seaside.
Owl, Lion, Whale, and Butterfly.

"It comes to our knowledge.
Our death is at hand.
For our brother the Man
Has come to institute our end!"

"To the Fish of the Sea,
Have you seen,
A place where the Creator waits and sees?"
"I am afraid Dear Elite We have not seen.
The place of a thousand dreams."

"You creatures of the land.
Have you seen this place,
Untouched by Judas the man?"

"We must say that our sight is bad.
For all our lives we hid from man."

"Then those of the sky.
Have you seen this place?
 For now is our time."

All the creatures stood and stared.

Until at last the Eagle dared.
"I have seen such a place from my upward flights.
Untouched by Man with glorious life!"

"Take wing my friend.
Do not travel alone.
Who will also go to the throne?"

While others stood in fear
The rat did come near.

"Your strengths have made you clean.
Ascend upon the wing.
We will see you in seven mornings."

By the Seventh Day
The Creatures were all in dismay.
Until at last.
The Wolf picked up.
A curious scent far away.
"The disciples have come on this very day."

The Eagle landed.
No rat descended.
Every creature made no sound.
All gazed with trepidation.
Until the Lion Spoke.
"What is the news,
You have brought forth?"

The Eagle praised,
"I have seen marvelous things.
Where all animals rejoice and sing.
Praises to the King."

"Where is the Rat?"
The Owl did who!

"The rat did stay.
So, my message is clear today."

With a flutter of mighty wings.
The Eagle lowered his head.

Thousands of hooves clattered.
All the birds sang.
For the creature sent was an Immaculate Lamb.
With peace and wisdom
And the heart of Ram
It would teach them a path
To the Promised Land.

TESTED

Naked is my open heart.
Elude the pain.

Our love's demise,
Is shared venom.
Say farewell.

The rage within my soul,
Thus, turning to gold.
When love becomes mythical.

Like dreams of Black Pegasus.
Or Rainbow Fish.

Time will stop the beating
Intervals of my heart.

TAINTED PROPHECY

Starved before my birth.
Set a fire to be lit.
In the bottom,
Of some loathsome pit.

A fate from heaven.
Bring your justification and scorn.
To my feet.
I dare none shall over compete.
With the demise and revenge.
Of my heart.

I am exhilarated.
The world is confused.
To my agenda.

Is it a crown of thorns?
Or merely a purse of jewels?
I will not burn.
I feel alive.

SOME THINGS

Some things seem so perfect.
Lotus flowers.
Spring Icicles.
A broken Whiskey Bottle.
Empty pack of cigarettes.

Tell me if you could?
That I am wrong
On such Matters of the heart?

Can you see?
Truly!
Are you aware?

The chasing of the wind.
A blanket of infamy
To cover our depression.

Judge when I say.
That love is so pure.
Perfect.
Like summer Shadows.
The screech of a hawk.
Grant me this truth.

A voice of soothing.
From the masses that sing.
A shower of mercy,
For the eternal unclean.

Take hold of these words!

Make this your day to cry!
Latter eve to laugh.
Tomorrow.
What will it bring?

SHAME

Shut the doors
On those who hurt you.
They say.
Walk where they walk
No more.

They also cry.
Just because they hurt me.
I should watch them die?

A cry for help
They wallow in their Shame.
Even though.
Hearts stay cold.
I will wipe my enemies' tears.
Before they dry.

SINKING

Kisses do scold,
A restless soul.
Narrative is my heart,
As it speaks to you.

God given is love.
Seen in tears from doves.
Shallow is the man.
Scant for loveless abuse.

The young shine.
Your heart is mine.
Yield yourself,
To my undoing.

Our rain is now snow.
Harbored feelings do grow.
Your roses will always bloom.
In my garden.

RUMORED FAME

Crossing over
Indeed is a place I Choose.
Whatever was before
Proves a relic photograph.
Trapped in this lifeless frame.
Which some call remains
Of traceability.

Oh I still exist.
Not just a mere shadow.
Or a mindless blur.
My name is known
 As a questionable word.

It is so quiet.
In the middle of the sea.
That is where I will be.

There is a fire looming,
Between this heart and soul.
Fame will eventually be sold.
As a priceless treasure.
Or a mere fool's gold.

AFFLICTED

Eyes so profound.
Call your name.
Sleep!

Clasp the hand.
Affliction is bleak.
Cry thy name…
Sleep!

I wish to speak with you
My Brother.
I pray for your soul.
Sleep.

OPEN REQUEST

One desolate somber hour,
I came to dance with rain.
It was Sunday.
When the world is most always tranquil.
Oh! How the wind played harmony
For such an intimate dance.

The sun came to enjoy the festival.
After the rain ceased to enjoy my mood.
The little birds flew from the heavens.
Just to see
Enjoy they did.
This I knew.

The sun tipped his rays.
As it left for its resting place.
The moon appeared.
With her entourage of stars.
Who poised on every beam,
Shone forth.
Before Sunday
Had become Monday
Alone I was no more.

ONE SIDED THINKING

No frame.
Black Portraits.
Shadow Images,
Speak.

Cringed vengeance.
Reverent promenade.
Ominous love.
A human satire.

Jeweled crown.
Enchained words.
Dusted existence.
Lies a friend.

Cowardly hatred.
Haunted lives.
Red Soil.
Earthly parade.

VI

On this rainy day.
You looked my way.
All the things I have done.
Still wreak havoc and stay.

Eyes withdrawn
You look at the sky.
For no reason why.

I often blame myself.
For lack of strength.
The familiar words of the tongue,
Mean nothing.

Years of deception
Promises,
I failed to keep.
We selfishly,
Will not let you see.
Th real inside of everything.

For years of possibilities.
I selfishly.
Would not let you see.
The truth inside of me.

I awoke to the sound,
Of the heart.
Wicked tears.
It was the first time.
I heard you cry.

On this Rainy day
I finally realized…
Why!
Wished myself.
A place to die.

So today I stand
To leave my pity.
With more rain.

OH SILLY ME

Is it fair for me to say?
That when you look my way.
I brighten your cloudy day.

Or is it right for me?
I am sure you will agree.
That our love
Was meant to be!

We gaze into each other's eyes.
Not sure whether to laugh or cry.
Before we can decide.

Oh I cannot stop rambling.

Smiles cross our glowing faces.
Where was I?
I must have mentioned.
That you are mine.

No thought stays,
More than a moment.
Work remains undone.
No rain or mud
Could destroy this mood.
I cannot stop
Loving you!

What were you saying?
Some words seem mute to me.
For my life is like a dream.
Oh Silly me.

MY GOD

My God
I have seen it.
Felt it
Not just an onslaught of death.
Rekindled the first light.
Place of tears.

Burning down the vineyards
Next will be the Great Pavilion

Rush hour.
I am emancipated.
By this day.

Unblemished by lost prophecy.
Not damned…
Well not quite yet.
Definitely.
Misunderstood.

Such a coward I have become.
Loathsome and fearful.
Which is honorable?

Holding a blade to my very neck.
Not that it would ever come to that.

Just a second…

Listen to this.

It feels so good to run.

NEVER FADE AWAY

Tailored suits
Gator shoes.
Cotton snow.
Southern blues.

Take a day.

Fight!

Wail!
Just an old blues, harmonica.

Duped?

Fear truly at Liberty.
They seek only
The supernatural anarchy!

Shuffle step.

Piece of the Apple Pie.

They Lie.

They Lie!

Just a couple of Good-Old Boys.

Drinking and smoking.
To Liverpool dreams.
Never fade away.

Rolling down a fiery Lady.

They seek out soldiers.
For Babylon's Revolutionary army.

MYSTERY MAN

Do your thoughts?
Hold many lies.
You walk with pride.
While many died.

Come for me.
With your twisted grin.
Drenched in sin.
You travel in.

So do not come.
To see our end.
I am free to live again.

Mystery Man!
I know your name.
Mystery man.
I know your game.

We search for light.
But in our minds.
So many white lines.
I watch for signs.

Stand and be still.
For in the dark.
Demons talk.

At night I pray.
For a way out.
But in doubt.
You cut me out.

Mystery Man!
Your countless souls.
Mystery man!
Outside my door.
Mystery Man!
I hold a gun
Mystery Man!
Our time has come.

DADDY

My Daddy told me,
That you cannot see race.
There is no difference.
Between a black or white snake.
They both bite.
That ain't right.
Let me tell you,
How to fight!

I fell so low,
Drugs, shame, pain, and sickness.
My life fell quickly.
One spring afternoon
My mind snapped.
Morning news…

I burnt my Daddy's home
Not that I was mad.
But a devil phoned.
My brain went a whirl.
Spell cast.
Oh Yeah.

Now everyone in town.
Knew My Daddy was Brown.
Heard of how one son died.
Hanging from a porch.

Had a daughter die,
Of loss of breath.
His youngest boy.
Arrest after arrest.

He hardly ever cried.
Until he heard I almost died.
After a failed suicide
All because I was chased.
By the other side
That ain't no lie.
Still looking for that caller.
With that spellbinding voice.

Please…
Tell me why?
You stood with me
When so many,
Could not hear.

Daddy tells why!

Blacks and whites
Don't try enough,
To shake hands.
Why do they fear us?
Why do we fear them?
Will racism truly ever end?
My son you are alive.
Change them.

NULL & VOID

My years were my enemy.
Which had no discontent.
I was forlorn and vulnerable,
To shield my grief.

It was my hopes.
That escorted me to you.

Forget what is called the past.
Or those you knew.
From long ago.

For the few that are found.
I am content to say welcome…

For those that are damned!
I yearn to say.
I miss you.

IMMORTAL BOUT

They bleed?
Yes!

Even fear one,
So small as me.
The trigger of time.
Dust-engaging saga.

No longer mere mortals.

Proverbs in such prodigal bout.

Gratis!
I cry…
From broken window frames.
The Ludus was a true game.
The Key was my distinction!

Celestial Orchids.
Be master of this realm.
The calling of death.
An Angel dares to wear black.
The dragon steals white.
My enemy is blood brother
To them both.

I fear them not.
For I was leant both
Shield and sword.
To My cause.

As I struggle
With the concept,
Of
Mortal being.

MIND GAME

It is a mind game to realize.
The power to be free.

I walk this place.
High on life.
In spite of strife.

Call me a fool.
Or a fiend.
But deep down inside.
You know what I mean.
A jungle of fears.
 Mixed with tears.
It's time to get past
These lonely years.

So we dance a new form of Hip Hop.
Jungle beats to move your sounds.
Get down
Get down
Get down

Know I am tripping
Now I am flipping.
Let's just start living.

Let go of the dope,
And other things.
Hypocritical strife
Get a new change on life.
Grab hold of this.

It feels so right.
Specially tonight.
Who cares the color,
From white, black, or green.
These words are meant
To set you free.

It's time to break into
A new place of energy.

I opened the mystic door.
For all those broken souls
The poor
Let's explore
A new realization
Forget segregation
Hesitation?
You know you want to see
The other side.

Not on your street drug high.
That only brings lies.

So we dance a new form of Hip Hop.
Jungle beats to move your sounds.
Get down
Get down
Get down

Know I am tripping
Now I am flipping.
Let's just start living.

MOURNFUL SCARS

I allocate you,
To be on the elevation,

Of the offended
Or victimized.

While lovers play.
Here you are at the house.
To touch or kiss…

Or
Others can implement.

Scream!
I will not tell.
Just memorize it.
She calls it purgatory.
He just sees Hell.
If they could only see Heaven.
As well.

LOST IN THOUGHT

I fear myself.

For I am lost.

Nightmarish cinemas.

Overplayed songs.

Teachers' words.

Fill my head.

To no end.

I cry myself

To sleep at night.

Am I still a man?

Who will wipe my tears?

When I realize.

I am alone.

Hatred is the science.

Which turns hearts,

To stone.

V

We are a piece of tearful time!

Exhausted and absent.

A wasted mind.

Living like mice to scurry.

Try to see…

Would you like to be with me?

Careful now…

Yielding love.

I am a river of ancient blood.

Telling no lies.

Running games.

Would you like to know my name?

Shhh!

We are gifts.

Placed as slaves.

Acquired

Finished

Sent away!

Generosity.

Limited time

Rally forth.

My words are not kind!

See me!

Want me!

Take me down.

Try to burn my soul

Into the ground.

We are life.

We are Preacher's Shame.

I just want my real name.

LAYERED CONQUEST

I must feel this again.

Not the rapier or the pedestal.

I need to feel.

The storm.

The rain.

So long drawn out, this melee.

I have not rested for so long.

I am the victor.

A cornerstone of this world.

Belongs to me.

A truth of all things.

That have passed.

A metal of valor.

For the mortified.

Dearest strife.

What have you truly,

Brought to me?

I am near the dark place

Once again…

The voices calling.

My Christian Name

To choose!

I will hold on to me.

I will not surrender.

To the folly…

Of

Slavery

Too much.

I have seen.

Complete desire.

To destroy.

Rigid,

Is my empathy.

Admonished,

Is my core.

Alive the cordial.

Hard line flash.

Saccharine vengeance.

Known

As my freedom.

LAST WORDS OF THE RICH MAN

I am busted.
No fight left in these hands.
These mistaken days of danger.
Have taken the toll.
On this dying man.

Too weary to run.
My days are done.
A rotting corpse.
Under a hateful sun.

I gave myself.
To a world of greed.
I took a piece.
It began to seed.

I am tired.
No more tears to cry.
My grave has been dug.
Too burned out for suicide.

So do not ask why
Or
Of whom.
Or do not assume.
That I am doomed.
I have purchased my own tomb.

But spare me a dime.
Make me a buck.
Shut your mouth!
I don't need your pity.
I am ashamed.
I missed your love

LAST NIGHT OF THE THIEF

VERSE 1

Wishes of peaceful days
Are slowly slipping away.
Yet I do not feel enslaved.
I do not feel afraid.

That makes me crazy.
In some,
Tormented way.
Things of past days.
Still linger like screams.
True street soldiers.
You know what I mean.

I really do not fit in.
Except for the shadows,
Of the street.
Who really cares?
Or even tries?
My mind filled
With so much bullshit.
Pride dancing with lies.
The attorney of the lonely.

Sleepless nights.
Has made his case.
Yet I have nothing more,
That I can take.
My Soul is slashed and torn.
For a moment.
I see the open door.

CHORUS

When will God finally,
Hear my cries
This world is all lies.
Nothing but lies
Yet try to believe me.
I tried!
A witchdoctor cursed me
Last time I died.
When will the light.
Bring peace to my soul.
My blood mixed with warriors.
Before I was born.
Michael!
Can you hear me?
Please hear me!
These fuckers fear me.

VERSE 2

I hit the streets
Driving fast.
No fear of police.
They have no wrath.
I hear footsteps of doom.
I know the war is coming soon.
I push the peddle to the metal.
I hear the whisper of the wind.

Through cracks in my door,
Thoughts of wives,
Girlfriends, and former whores.
Some bitch has marked me.
I know this for sure…

CHORUS

When will God finally,
Hear my cries
This world is all lies.
Nothing but lies
Yet try to believe me.
I tried!
A witchdoctor cursed me

Last time I died.
When will the light.
Bring peace to my soul.
My blood mixed with warriors.
Before I was born.
Michael!
Can you hear me?
Please hear me!
These fuckers fear me.

VERSE 3

My baby's asleep at home.
I put it out of my mind.
Just for a time.
They have done no wrong.
Now feel the words of this Psalm.

No Love.
No peace
Just revenge and all that shit.
This world order has got me in a fix.
What have they put me in.
Let this moment be for a soulful deal.
Thoughts of steel and broken movie reels.

I feel this shit deep.
My dreams have become valid.
It's finally given chase.
These hiders think I am blind.
Three cars pull up without haste.

CHORUS

When will God finally,
Hear my cries
This world is all lies.
Nothing but lies
Yet try to believe me.
I tried!
A witchdoctor cursed me
Last time I died.
When will the light.
Bring peace to my soul.
My blood mixed with warriors.
Before I was born.
Michael!
Can you hear me?
Please hear me!
These fuckers fear me.

VERSE 4

I turn on the radio
Gangster, Gangster plays.
Even though it's been five years.

I have tried to be good.
You know
Live life like the rest.
But the nation of colors.
Rarely find true rest.

The word is that we are free.
That equal is not blind.
These damn,
Matrix-like rules.
Are so unkind.
The thug is gone
So unkind.

My only crime.
Is that I can see.
Death is present.
Look to the sea.
Gravestone's an address.
Dirt hearth for the likes of me

JOSEPH WEEPS

He cries for his brothers.
Deep within the depression.
He weeps.

Without knowing.
Why the coat of many colors?
Has brought him shame.
Disgrace.
Such power is fear.
The weeping.
Eleven to twelve.
Are his callous tears.

He dares not curse them.
As his own anger deep within,
The callous pit.

Yes curse them?
Send them into the abyss?
Feel for them no more?

He can only pray.
Between tears.
Can they not see his humiliation?

See me in this pit!

God does know of his pain.

Enslaved.
How is this justice?

Pray for your brothers.
Dares to challenge,
the last of his humanity

Joseph Weeps

Palaces and Pyramids?
Rings of power?
So close.

I am
Cannot choose between.
The silence.
Or the screams.
His coat is now
Bloodstained.
Tainted with lies.

Joseph weeps.

IV

Is this more than time?

It is aptness.

I am so close to this psychosis.

A vision only.

One!

The world.

I have found no life!

She hates me.

She despises me.

It's over.

Like clear fathoms

Of indecisions.

I am at this moment.

No more a thief than a fool.

Hear the rage!

It is overwhelming me.

Like lambs to slaughter.

I am becoming so angry.

Let it be?

No, forget that!

Let it take hold.

Shout out the pain.

How sad.

How intense.

Look at me.

This man.

This place.

It is a lie.

A complete do over.

This I will try.

INSANITY

I sought out deception.
The illusion?
Of such hysteria.
Just annoyed notions.
More than capital.
Or moral fiber.

An insight into the mind.
Filled with unresolved hate.
Abysmal… Torment.

The view.
Ah yes,
The view.
Would cause some to grow,

Completely insane.
I have tried to remain unchanged.
For this psychosis is unhurried.
By the few mortals that care…
The eyes just stare.
So unaware

INTIMATE PENITENTIARY

Give me a den.
A hole to Escape.
See the flame.
Put out of sight.
The inferno…
Conversing.
With no one.
Exhausted and fearful.
Of the thereafter.

Just a member.
A seed in the field.
My heart is kept in a cold box.
Faith?
A grass blade.
A water drop.

Keep the head high.
Death is feared.
Leave me
Alone now.

Injudicious,
Mortified,
Dishonored,
Intimate.

What have we done?

IMAGINARY FRIEND

So good to see you again.
Like a gentle breeze,
That comes to kiss my soul.
How long will you stay?
My worst pain.
Is when you go away.

The next time you hide.
Please avoid the sun.
The clouds lie to me.
They like to watch me run.

Do not sit with the moon.
It causes great jealousy.
Sheltering quiet shadows.
To disguise you from me.

Just come and whisper in my ear.
The words I will hear.
Bringing forth
Shallow tears.
When no one is near.
It all becomes
Painfully clear.
My Imaginary Friend.

SONGS

I stood in the middle
Of an open field.
Broken but feared.
They cheered.

So timely was my exit.

Days pass on.
To a place of songs.

I am strong
Skulking past.
Lonely thieves.
On my back
Hung iniquity.

Only to be chased…
Mocked.

In the middle of the field.
My heart would heal.
The moonbeams cheer.
The crowd was not real.

II

Focused on quivering skin.
Now the bitter begins
Cornered by the dawn.
Let me go!

Kill it!
Let it not escape.
Then awake.

Anger leads me to your door.

Slipped.
Into the whispering belt.
I wait there.
Desiring for the full edge.

I am not a perfect man.
The door is locked.
I will come again,
And again.

Each day.
I will check the lock.

Careful not to sleep.
I will flood your dreams.
With my hate.
Until at last you let me in.
Confronted by absolute horror.

No!
You are standing there.
My deeds do dare!
You are aware.
Just shut the door.
The last fight

I am moving on.

I FEEL NOTHING

Outside my window.
I stare.
I chained myself.
To this fragment.
In this place od screams.
Repulsion!
Just to hide from the toll.

They wanted me dead.
Too much to give.
So, I say here…
Knowing nothing.
Finding love.
From the mentally Ill.

The nurses here are ok
Sometimes it is fine to be sick.
They say I just need rest.
They just do not know.
All the truth behind it.

It doesn't matter right now!

I have different roommates.
Some come in.
Covered in pain.
No rain for their sorrows.
While others are here.
Just to wail and bawl.
At the sprawl of humanity!

One was from Laos.
He was a monk
This western world was way too much.
Even for him.

Yet we grieve for others in our own way.
He cannot speak English.
So I teach him my way.

He teaches me to pray.
Meditate on love.
He prays for me at night.
The voices go away.

He picks up a bible.
He tells me to read.
A girl outside is crying.
As I lean into his small Buddhist chant.

Quiet!

An angel is with us.
I finally can sleep.
It has been so long
 Since I have slept.
So long!

HOURGLASS

I am the sand of the hourglass.
Dying pebble by pebble.
Grit by grit.
Until at last.
A solitary grain of sand sits.
Attached to the glass.

How is that my drowned life.
Became a resurrected energy.
With a twist of the wrist.
I am set free.
To start a new eternity.

I

Take me back.
Hold my mind.
I see you speaking.
You are mine.

We have sex.
 We can be.
Trapped within.
Rome's society.

The twisted words
Of the damned.
Could you really love?
Fellow Man…

We are!
They see!
We are only fantasy.

Souls placed
In colored corps.

To die!

Seems like assurance!

Guided by false prophets.
and tax man's greed.
I see you as the end of me.

HOW DO YOU SPELL BEATNIK?

Like jazz,
Playing in the distance.
Dark corners filled with smoke and haze.
Feel me
What is a Beatnik?

Don't call me Sampson or her Delilah.

It turns out to be like Sonny and Cher.

Then I have just run to that place.

Where is the Beatnik?

Dollar shoes, Deep blues.
Figuring out the next design.
Poetic lines.
With ancient wine.

More like Bill and Hillary?

That question mark is placed for reason.

When did you see a Beatnik?

Quantum leaps.
And barred gates.
Feel me. Roses sliced with flames.
Damn! They tried to change.
I hear the drum.
The mixed, mash string,
Yeah that's the kiss.

HUMAN FOLLY

Listen to this absolute sound…

If you dare!

Along heathen scripts.
Pagan roses
Laid to rest.
Locked my doorways.
Stolen keys.

This journey.
So vigilant in expansion.
Callous.
Dark.
Alone.

This is my resting place.
For the transgressions.
They marvel at unpunished mortals.
My sins are heard through tainted whispers.

A raven's black heart.
Enraged intentions.

Forgive me for my lust.
Hallways of broken glass.
My dreams of rain-filled streams.

Among the spirit world,
I am lost, stale and uninviting.
Infatuation
Sacrifice
Afflictions.

I am only human!

HIS PAIN

It is rotten flesh!
Numbness.
Deep within!
Not Love?
Just the pain
The reaping.
How does it feel?
To cry.
Just a whisper.

It's the partition,
From God.
That pains me most.
The fallen.
So pure and evil
Was the humiliation of one!

Now I see
The passion.
The rain.
The arousing.

It still hurts.
To find out most of us are cowards.
Terrified of the alter.
The circle is broken.
The cross is unbearable,
At times.

Would someone carry it for me.
For just a little while!

I will find a way. To heal.
Covered in shame.
I will rise to be,
Free and one,
With it all!

HAND QUAKE

These are my expressions
My judgments.
Of
Nightmares.
Scrolled
By
Scathing
Unmerciful hands.

With these two lucid limbs.
I grabbed.
I shattered.
Lifted disease to my bloodied lips.
Rubbed delicate skin.
With dirty fingertips.
Wiped the tears from sad, red eyes.
Broke bread with strangers.
Beat them on Hell's very door.
Climbed to the edge of Heaven.
Crawled along a neighbor's floor.

Stole the breath.
Of a few who cried.
Put them together.
Prayed to die.

FORGIVEN

Blind so Blind.
The laws of men.
Obliteration, terror, they guide.
Only through their eyes.

If you fall.
Your brothers will know.
Make you pay.
Lock you away.
Until they say.
Your crime is paid.

We are bastards.
Such that I see.
Abandoned and submerged.
I began to drown.

I paid the price.
With putrid disfigurement.
I try to battle with all my might.
For a new.
Resurrected life.

GOD CALLED FOR AN EAGLE

Speak for me!
Fisherman.
I hate the fish.
Streams of trout
Fields for the deer
Devils for the flames!

Quiet mist.
For the Dawn.
Snow for the mountaintops.
Woman for a man.

I asked for a gift.
That would make me stand.

Blanketed tears from
Spartan eyes.
Pain to his ears.
Fear in is heart.
Awe from his mouth.

We smiled deeply.
With a brush of his hair.
So gentle a gift.

Yet I hate the fish?

Stretch out your wings.
My little friend.

With my lips.
I give you the wind and breeze.
To the eagle.
He gave you everything.

FIRST TIME

I asked her how it felt?

The first time.

She said, "Fuck you!"

Then she said they call it popping the cherry!

Creatures showed up at the door.

With howls of deceitful pleasures.

It was thwarting and tactless.

Virgin princess stuck in a game.

She did not know.

I felt her humiliation.

Then replied.

"I didn't mean your thrashing!"

"But the first time with me?"

She smiled and cried all at once.

She leaned on me.

To take that division away.

Make it last forever.

Was her intention.

To hide was my initial.

Finding the ambient place in it all.

FORTIFIED REPENTANCE

No love today.
Just pain
Exhausted from paying
This porthole toll.

No Gazing.
At the Cadence signs.
Painted across
Back Alleyways

Cursing the humanity
Feeding the positive.
Screwing the negative.

Man!
The dealers of death
Need a place to hide.
Vermin?
Let alone Masters of disease!

Inhale now!
Exhale!

ENDLESS MYTHS

I could have been the elite.
Where people would say.
"There goes a Man
With influential hands."

Somewhere along the line.
I ended up on some far-off peak.
Between might and meek.
Possibly a freak?

Nothing is for sure.
As a few will attest.
Indeed, Heaven knows of rest
Conclusive jest.

No Memory goes unmoved.
Sleep often becomes death.
In the cold I see breath.
Endless Myths.

ESCAPING

The rest of the world.

Stand still!

So tranquil.

Do you dare?

I will carry you there.

In this portrait of time.

We can try,

Intimate, alluring tastes.

Sharing.

Caliginous foundations.

To be alone,

With you.

Where would you choose to be?

I would take the farthest sea.

A place of wonders.

Full of Majesty.

We would sit.

Wait…

Watching the sunrise.

I close my eyes.

Beginning to cry.

Knowing my sin.

Is the reason why.

DRUG OUT

Let me be the first
To find some shit.
Tired of white-collared hypocrites.
I am making this hit.
Like a drill to my head.
I am killing so many robotic-like minds.
Leaving so many drugged and behind.

Left for dead!

Whatever the game?

Fuck the fame!

World's about to change.
So, I am starting the flames.
As the last finally become the first.
It will be the man that I hurt.

A revolution has begun.
Watch the rising of the sun.

How many screams from city ghettos?
Let me say hello,
With a raised fist.
I am about to turn up the shit.

Never mind poetic lace.
I see the devils fall on their face.
I am rising above your fates.
Your lessons of prison.

I will not listen.

DREAMSCAPE

A place of wonders.

I give you bird's wings.
Sailor days.
I see you challenged.
Caught up in the moment.

Please take time.
To Unwind.
Believe me.
I have travelled here.
Many times!

We are free to be.

Stoned Metaphors
Of
Reigning plots.

Centurion's
Armed escort.

I am no more or less
A
Major.
Or even a king!

Nor Prince.

I am a citizen

My dreams mean
More to me.

Than titles

and greed.

YOU WISH

You wish.
You could live out your dream
Not those thoughts
Of the rich and famous.
But the Phantasms that scare you.
That hurt you.
Love you.
Freak you
Shame you.

Yes!

Those fantasies.
That give you power
That are purple, pink, and blue.

You know that dream.
Where you run naked and free.
Not a wasteland Desert.
More like Adam and Eve.
In a tropical forest of rain.
Filled with Flora and Fauna.
Where whispers are always heard.

That is the mental image.
No news
Or Sinners.
No Square Houses.
No lies.
Forget concrete roads,
Fast cars and suicide.

Just a spawned
Utopian high
Where I am alive!
Alive?
With a peaceful Sigh.

DEVASTATION

It stood!
It stared!
Into my fading eyes.

When it took
My Lifeless body.
Leaving a decaying soul.
I have never.
Felt such cold.

Withered and tragic.
I still survived!

Wasted and scorned.
Of vast sins.

This dormant heart.
Kept me in the act.
Of
Pagan Institutions.

I held death's unreeling hand.
Its taunting grip.
Excommunicating
This once strong man.
Devastation.

CENTURIES APART

Let us return
To Bronze,
Silver,
And Gold.

Where wealth and power.
Was more than sold.

Where I could be King!
By my own hand.
Not forced to live by,
Fellow man.

This is the time that I seek.
With the air undefiled
And death to the meek.
When people adhered to their own.
Kingdoms and knew nothing of thrones.

The sword and shield.
The pike and spear.
The shriek and pain of the battlefield.
Are the song and music of my heart.
A shame being born centuries apart.

DEAR BROTHERS

No spoken words.
To accusers
No Tears for believers.
Gold for children.
Love for oneself.
Stand in this world.
Especially those fallen from grace.
Look for your inner integrity.
Such beauty.
So much pain.
Behind prison walls.

Fallen the mind.
Vanishes like a villain.
In the mountains.
Inner roads from the past.
Where lies run off.
I fear that voice.
In all splendor.
It gives no rest.

I did have a kiss.
Once so long ago.
How much I hate time.
Struggle to fight.
Hold on to silver linings.
Dreaming of someone
Else's pot of gold.

A short verse echoed.
From Adam's earthly Shadow.
To a poor slave's grave.

Keep my mind free.
From the potter's day.
Hold on just a little longer.
Brother!
I have been there.

CARESS

My core holds the secrets
To pleasures rarely seen.

It is here.
You will find.
Trustworthy deed.

Chatter amidst
Laughter's essence.
You will find me.

Before this tale.
Comes to a close.
The hollow shell of emptiness.
Which is called human sacrifice.
What I call love.

Caress.

BROKEN HEARTED

There is a road.
That has countless dreams.
Always travelled.
Rarely seen.

Hold my hand.
As we walk.
But do take care.
To let others, talk.
Why is it so
Many millions
Of
falsifiers?

Outnumber
The righteous!

FREEDOM?

The intoxication
In the valley view.
Of Sad Pedestrians
Occupations can leave us so alone.
Without purpose.
At least the sun shines forth.

The circle broken and charred.
Immoral of the curtain.
The path and order.
Which demands contract
Unwashed freedom.

This is the tale.
Sheer power.
Hiding within.
Foundations of the earth, wind, water, and fire.
Uncovered balance of the lavish.
A key hidden within the battlefront.
Of such elements.
Is worth the penalty I Pay.

They have taken my blood.
Four vials, with a dull needle!
For unspeakable tests.
I have no Idea.

Freedom?

CALCULATED SUCCESS

Lucky Seven
Four leaf clover.
No chance to help thee.
Real human satire.
Brought tears of pain.
To my eyes.
It was a pledge.
That I will never die.

New generations.
Think themselves,
As earthly gods.

They have reached space.
Created
Gigantic might.

Yet they cannot stop
Beating the wife.

Dreams of control
Talks of change.
Forgotten names
Of
The Son.
They spit upon the cross

Man is a blind soldier.
That has not realized
He is lost.

SHIPWRECKED

I was left unaided.
Along a seaside.
That is where.
My prayers died.

Oh, so Sad
Just too wrong.
Shipwrecked.
The rocky shore.
Has become my grave.
Waves.
Winds.
Salt eating into my bow
The Feeling.

PLAGUED

Tenderly
I Kiss you.
Can I honestly say?
You need me!
Like drifting sand.
Needs dancing rain.
Withered grass.
Desires,
Raging wind.
As I need you.

I Beseech and look.
For something new.
Not in others
But in you.

I am caught!
Plagued!

Like cold days
To cloudless nights.
We are coupled.
We have squandered tears.
Spent on distant fears.
Left By Painful years.

BITTER REVELATIONS

It was red wine
That I drank
Fire that I consumed.
It was not strong enough.

For what you might ask.

I was weak when the children cried
For help.
But I tried.
Asleep when the villains came.
When the heroes died.
Everyone
Knew my name.

WHEEL OF BLOOD

We set races and faces.
Blood and rain.

Like vinegar and water.
As the crow flies to the brain.
I feel abhorrence and fury.
Running through my veins.
A riot of scriptures.
Attacking my name.

Here me now!

A lost tribe of Africa
Mixed with Native song.
A white man's name.
What the hell is going on.

We battle the man.
With song and written word.
Too Bad
So Sad.
I stand in a pool of blood
As they call my ancestors.
A thief on a cross

Demand that the man be judged.
We can move on.

BACK OF THE CLASS

Paper colored walls.
Called Education.
The school is small.
I sit alone
At the back of the class

Doll for a teacher
You know the type.
You sit upright.

.

Dead eyes open.
She was hard on me.
Caught in an earlier time.
She would separate me.
Scapegoat for the class.

Years noted.
I feel no anger or regret.
She was just a figurehead.
Of some forgotten time.

The bell ringing
Time to go home.

She scowls.
As I walk out the door.
Then says.
"Have a nice day!"
"Go straight home."

ROCKSTAR

It is so lucid
Such a man.
So brawny and zealous.
He is music
His brood are far from his obscure reach.
Like chaos in falling snow.

All are enslaved.
Within footsteps.
To his mind's eye.

Mass hindered by the real.
Broken mirror.
A segment of rules engaged.

He's alone most nights.
Can you feel his rage?

A REFUGE FOR MY SOUL

I searched for a resting place.
Beyond the trees.
I traveled the ocean breeze.
I searched…

How it hurt.
To know,
That snow comes and goes.
My heart had locked the door.

Farewell to the sun.
Greetings to the moon.
How soon I will know of you.

I wept last night.
Felt tears of affliction.
Upon my numb cheek.
I wiped sweat
From my blistered brow.
My soul has a haven now.

A MOURNFUL RESOLUTION

Remind me to call you tomorrow.
To see if you are still alive.
Last night I had a dream.
That the entire world had died.

All that had laughed and danced.
To the wrath of sinners' games.
Felt only pain.

The Devil Rejoiced.
By burning flames.
His entourage
Applauded his name.

God stood Alone
On his heavenly throne.
The Angels cried
Not wanting to sin
The Almighty had decided on things.

That no one was to be called servant.
For those Created in his image had let him down.
Fears that had gone on for thousands of years
Had turned to tears.
Such my dream feared.

YESTERDAY

He follows me
As darkness is second to light.
He rests on my soul.
As I walk.
He lurks!
Behind every nook,
Boulevard.
Ready to defile
My new name.

He emerged from the mist of my time.
Never before seen.
My age has made me prisoner
To his devotion.

Raped and abused by life.
I hear him sneer.
My grave seems my only rest.
How long can you run, he asks?

XXX

The scent of treasure

Take it blue.

Hushed tons of Energy.

Dancing Women

Broken yolk.

Forged enlightenment

Quiet eyes.

Absolute astral bodies.

Say goodbye!

Shame on you.

Friendship thing.

I loathe you!

As much

As I love myself.

Which isn't much!

QUIET PLACES

It is not what they said.

That made me take note.

Or what one did

To make me retort.

To such accusations.

I concluded…

There was a plot.

When I heard them

.

Jesting for me to scream.

Provoking me to run.

Can it be said?

That the few who know.

Refuse to speak.

Is it true?

That the illusions

Of this so-called agony.

Goes unnoticed.

In quiet places.

PROVERB

Share a vision of independence with fiends.
I will show you an inception of terror
Never before seen.
Take time to run with villains
It will cause your knees to bleed and splinter.
Like an ax through a sapling.

When you begin to dwell in the night.
Do not be afraid to dance.

I have joy.
Where you have dreamed.
Seen the shaman behind the purple cloud.
Gazed into the white eyes of the Alive.

When you search to find me.
Avoid the lost near-light,
Of the hunter's moon.
Search for clues from stagnant air.
In the nostrils of inept days of yore.

When we surpass.
The flames of the blazing star.
You might find a lingering trail.
To that unique place.
Know as Kingdom come.
Or if you prefer.
The Golden Gates.
Of
Heaven.

PHANTOM CREATION

Awaken!

I am a luminary.
Triumph into my distorted past.
I have freedom.
Wouldn't it be interesting to find?
A brilliant worship,
In amongst the breathing dull.
Wandering back and forth.

I have been able to survive,
A vision or two.
I even had time to awaken a dead man.
From the achievement.
Of a lifelong sleep.

I must make it clear to you.
I am flesh.
Immaculate psyche.

A real secret.
It was in my creation of my youth.
Yes!
In my early days.
I came to dance with rain.

How sweet was her disposition.
That I find it impossible,
To forget her.

It was also around the same time
That I began a new song.
It was so ancient, yet so new.
I had forgotten,
Its dawning.
But I still remember.
Its gentle end.

POWER

The vision
Of Everlasting control.
Steaming from a gentleman.
Squandered imagining.
Reaching into the pinnacle
Of Life.

Might is found increased.
Soiled hands become clean.
Seen in every invigorated line.
Sagacious cross.
Moving sacred times.

Through the hearts of Masters.
Setting greater nations apart.

It is why I sleep.
It is why I hate.
To rise as the cock crows.
I am searching for integrity.
Such a word gone amiss.
Such a hard card dealt.
Such is power.
To oneself!

PEEK THIS

Peek this.
The few of you.
Who merely trudge.
With vagabonds and harlots.
Away your essence drifts.
Out of reach.
Internal.
You are left with sleep
For hungry dogs reap.
At fleshy heaps.

I bid you
This meager timid farewell.
On your trip to Hell.
Too bad there are those who fell.
Many I knew well.

I carry the sadness.
On my way to the grave.
Turned away
Lost my way
Now forced to live
Another day.

PAWN

Kiss and damned.
You made me love you!

Forcing me unto the game table.
Yes, the Chess board
Spinning me round and round.

Pawn to Knight
This Rook.
Has foundation.
For such fear of my knowledge.
I dare not stay.

Knowing my purpose
Was of innocence
I chose the path of such fire.

Knowing I can see.
You leave me no choice.
To cringe and run.
At the coat of arms.

Blood has no end.
To the line of this page.

PAIN

Undertone of the underworld
In the heated night.
Dragons' inferno.
Within my soul.
Terrified Angels no longer sing
But scream the Devil's Toll.

Focused and hateful.
I regret your recent love.
I searched for newfound happiness
Was exposed,
Deranged,
And drugged.

If Pain only had a cure.
For broken hopes and dreams.
There would be no memories.
Of how thing used to be.

I am partial to retribution.
I set in motion.
My mounting pride.
Watching you from a distance.
While others pass us by.

PARTY SOUL

Hey, a party is going on.
Let's jump onto this song.
Girls making the floor hop.
Let the Ice melt.
I have a vision of orgies
Coming on.
OH AH AH AH.

You like it like that.
Bad Boys.
Always.

Hide away in apartments.
They are new to you.
Music playing.
Getting you in the mood.

Everybody playing rich.
Drug dealers.
Pimps.
Want to be Imps.
Party girls moving hips.
Painted lips.
OH AH AH AH.

That's the formula
I am teasing you with it.

Come closer.
Oh that's right.
Sneaking out to the club.
On a Friday night.

Will it hurt
Maybe for a bit.
But you know you need it.
That is the trick.
OH AH AH AH.

Like a Wizard
You are bound to dwell
Even frigid girls
caught in the spell

Now let us feel it.
Mean it.
Hold it for a run.
Keep this feeling Going.
To the rising sun.
OH AH AH AH.

Now face your maker.
Come Sunday morning.
Hell bound to the sound
So so Sorry.

PAINTED MAN

How dark is your day.
As the religious mock his rise to claim,
his true name.
Dear Othello,
Or is it Black Jesus.

I hear the leaders laugh
at your existence.
So dark your hands
Spoiled by white women.
In unknown lands.

Dear Moorish kin.
I hear them cast lots upon your grave.
Suicide? Yes? No!
From being so beautiful.
How is the dawn?
Where is thy mystic purpose?
That demons in isolation
Can taste your very soul.
As spirits fight unseen battles.
To protect the sacred throne.

Do you hear faint whispers?
Of the departed…
As the control for mindful dreams.

Easing your very death.
Into unwanted dreams.

Lightning Source UK Ltd.
Milton Keynes UK
UKHW040623041222
413302UK00003B/117

9 781039 158733